Praise for

NOT YOURS TO KEEP

"Nature versus nurture is a question that has been debated for centuries. Just how much weight is given to genetic and biological influences versus those that come from social, economic, and environmental influences? My friend of nearly twenty years explores this debate in her debut memoir, *Not Yours to Keep*. The story explores Julie's life as an adoptee into a warm, loving, and somewhat affluent family, and then takes a twist once Julie meets her biological mother, Diana, and discovers the similar twists, turns, and fates that both she and Diana experienced. The story is thoughtful, kind, and at times very raw. Happily, I can attest that Julie had a very successful career in product and service sales and she and her husband Rob raised five children who are loving spouses and proud parents with highly distinguished professional careers. You will laugh, you may cry, and I'm sure you'll enjoy the interspersing of poetry written by Diana herself. Nature versus nurture . . . who knows? But I'm sure you'll simply delight in the emotionally rich lives of Agnes, Diana, and Julie."

—*Elizabeth Darragh, Retired Vice President*
of Marketing and Communications

"Julie traveled similar paths as Diana without ever meeting her until later in their lives. Nature and nurture both prove important. They endured a rollercoaster of challenges and came out whole and wiser and loved. I am blessed to call Julie a longtime friend."

—*Maggie Furlong, Retired Teacher*

"As an adoptee myself, I found Julie's memoir deeply moving and relatable. *Not Yours to Keep* explores the profound questions that often arise from adoption: Who are my biological parents? Why did they surrender me? What traits have I inherited from them? Julie answers these questions and more with honesty and insight. Having known her for seventeen years, I can attest to her thoughtfulness, reflection, and depth as a writer. Her book takes readers on a journey of joy, sorrow, and ultimately, an awakening to the strength and resilience of women.»

—Lori Lipten, Clinical and Humanistic Psychology, Author, Spiritual Guide

"What an inspiring and moving story! I have always admired Julie for the long and successful career she had and for being a strong leader that cared about the company, its people, and her family. Above all, I always appreciate that, whether good or bad, it was (and is) always the real her, and that takes a lot of courage. Julie's story not only tells the why but also puts things in a different perspective. Everyone has their story, and time together allows us to truly get to know another human being."

—Martin Meckesheimer, Director, Analytics and Innovation

"Having known Julie more than twenty-five years, it is no surprise to me that she would have the determination to find her birth mother while there was still time to make a positive connection to the benefit of them both. Julie has a bias to action and faces life and its twists and turns with an open heart and unflinching determination. It is easy to believe that she owes her character both to the parents that raised her and the woman that brought her into the world. Julie's story is an inspiration."

—Stephen DiRubio, COO

NOT YOURS TO KEEP

NOT YOURS TO KEEP

A Story About Adoption and the Strength and Resilience of Women

JULIE MELANSON

Published by Rooted in DAY Publishing

ISBN (print): 979-8-9992183-0-8
ISBN (ebook): 979-8-9992183-1-5

Book design and production by www.AuthorSuccess.com

DEDICATION

To the mothers who bring children into this world and make the hard decision to give them up so they can have a better life. To the mothers who raise those children, love them as their own, and create wonderful lives for them. To all mothers who work so hard to provide the best life they can for their children and family, whether they are single or married.

To my children and their spouses: Renee and her husband Lee, Kevin and his wife Maureen, Paul and his wife Radhika, Evan and his wife Laura, and Sam and his wife Kim, and my grandchildren: Mia, Meredith, Siana, Mackenzie, Asha, Declan, Kian, and Jack, who have created a supportive, loving, funny family that I enjoy every day. And, most importantly, to my husband and best friend Rob, who has been by my side for thirty years and has walked through life's journey with me hand in hand. We have been blessed with a beautiful family for which I am so thankful. And to my two Portuguese water dogs, Ome and Healy, who have laid by my side every day as I embarked on my writing journey. Thank you to all of you!

CONTENTS

PROLOGUE

N ot *Yours to Keep* explores some themes that no adoption
memoir has yet done.

What does the child owe the birth parent, if anything?
What if the reunion is joyous, but the relationship becomes
consuming? What if the birth mother wants nothing to do
with the child she bore? What does a birth mother owe to
the child she gave away? What is the impact of each mother
on the child? What about nurture vs. nature? How do the
families of the birth mother and adoptive parents manage the
relationship? Is there any sense of entitlement or resentment?

However difficult my path, I was as much a survivor as was
Diana. We did not see one another for fifty-one years, but I
believe that she had been my fierce and constant ally all along.

This is not just an adoptee's tale; it is a survivor's tale. Diana
began taking her blows at birth and would spend her life
chasing peace. I had nothing but peace for my first twenty
years, so I knew it was possible to regain it, however far gone
it seemed.

INTRODUCTION

What the other girls thought of the pretty little Irish girl, who had two parents but came in and out of the orphanage every several months, no one knew. Diana Sparbeck's parents dumped her in the Sarah Fisher Home outside of Detroit whenever they chose to separate. Her older brother went to her grandparents, her handicapped sister to an aunt, and Diana developed a lifelong dread of the backseat of cars; for her, they signified abandonment. Still, she begged the sisters at the home to keep her because the nuns were her family.

Diana learned elegance from her parents'—taste, even— but she was more influenced by her rougher Aunt Kate, who smelled of pot roast and perfume samples and admonished young Diana with, "The angels are deaf to your pissin' and moanin'. Get on with it!"

Diana was destined to be a nun, her parents told her, but in 1955, she was too mouthy, unafraid of drink, and unafraid of boys to join the holy orders.

Her cousin would recall that she was "sent away to a convent" at seventeen—the polite and Irish way of explaining away (without admitting to) an unwed pregnancy.

Diana's mother was scandalized by the pregnancy, doubly scandalized that the child was born of a rape. She shucked her staunch Catholicism and demanded that Diana abort the child. Diana defied convention (as she always would) and bore Kim Marie. She gave up the infant for adoption but ignored the custom that she would never see the child, and held her and cooed to her for an hour. It was painful, but there was some solace in knowing she would be at the Sarah Fisher Home, where Diana's parents would leave her during troubled times, awaiting adoption. She knew the love and the kindness the nuns would provide for her baby.

It was only a short six weeks before Kim Marie Sparbeck became Julia Marie Crombe. Agnes and Norbert Crombe had suffered for years, watching their extended family grow around them while they remained childless after the death of their firstborn, Therese Marie. After seven years, they adopted Julia Marie and named her after Norbert's mother. His parents migrated from Belgium, and his father, Julius, had passed when Norbert was six years old. It's only a year and a half after adopting their baby girl that they conceive John Joseph.

Julia (later called "Julie") came to believe that her father was a college professor, her mother a student, and their love a forbidden but beautiful thing; that being surrendered to an orphanage was a tragic but loving act on her mother's part. This appealed to her sense of romance, one she developed with her girlish love for the *Cinderella* story and for the professor/

student romance of *My Fair Lady*. She had a few details of her heritage; that her birth name was Kim Marie Sparbeck (she found that by snooping in a box of deeds and other family documents), and that she was half Irish and half French. She looked up the name "Sparbeck" in the phone book and found them plentiful around Michigan.

Finding her birth parents seemed unimportant to a girl who had grown up to feel special and wanted by her adoptive parents.

Still, as years pass, she wondered who her birth parents were every time she filled out a medical form and left question marks in the family history; when she gave birth to sons Kevin and Paul and wondered what traits (which skip generations) she was passing on; whenever people told her they had seen someone who looked like her. She did not resemble her adoptive family, but wondered as a girl singing in a school performance if a birth parent sat in the audience and watched her. She searched every crowd for a familiar face, one that mirrored her own. She never found it.

CHAPTER 1
FINDING DIANA: THE SEARCH

At age forty-seven, and eight years after having lost my mother, Agnes, I decided to search for my birth mother. I hired a professional search company, which turned up nothing in four years and closed my case. I came to believe that I was just not meant to know my history.

After some time, interestingly, my husband, Rob Melanson, and I were watching a program on TV about how much information you can learn about yourself now on the internet. The next morning, as we were sitting and talking on our farmer's porch overlooking the Merrimac River in Amesbury, Massachusetts, enjoying our Cape Codder cocktails, we decided to look and see what we could find out. Since I knew that my birth last name was Sparbeck, we were able to find a number of people with that surname in Michigan. We dug a little deeper and were able to see the ages and locations of many of the women. Finally, we settled on a woman named

Joanne Sparbeck and were stunned to find her phone number as well. Now what to do?

Later that day, I decided to take a chance and reach out to Joanne. As luck would have it, I got a voicemail that was pretty non-descriptive. Maybe it was the Cape Codders, but I left my name, Julie Melanson, and said that I was looking for health information, thinking I may be related to their family and that my intent was not to cause any issues or problems. There, it was done! My anticipation and anxiousness about receiving a return call was palpable, but as the next day came, and the next day, and the next, I started to believe I would not hear back from her. It was the fourth day after I left that message for Joanne, and I finally received a call back, not from Joanne but from her son, who told me that his mother had passed away. We spoke for a few minutes, and finally, it became clear to him that I was looking for a birth parent. He told me that he was sure it was not his mother, as she had married into the Sparbeck family in her twenties. He did share that his Uncle Jerry would be the one to speak to, as he had all the family history, and that he would call him and give him my contact information. I waited about three weeks with nothing from Uncle Jerry. I called Joanne's son back, and he said he would reach out to Jerry again. Within a day or so, Jerry contacted me. We shared information about ourselves, and I stated what I was looking for along with my intentions. Jerry suggested that we exchange pictures; he had a photo of Gertude Sparbeck, his aunt, that might be helpful. We connected the following week, and Jerry thought that there may be a connection. He asked if I would like for him to send me a family tree. "Of course!" I exclaimed. I was getting a little closer.

When I received it, Rob and I spent time going through the family tree and decided the most logical person that could be my birth mother was a woman named Diana Healy. I sent an e-mail to Jerry, and he asked that I do nothing until we could speak.

Jerry recalled that his cousin Diana Healy (formerly Diane Sparbeck) was "sent away to a convent" when she was seventeen. Diana had a tough childhood, including frequent stays at the Sarah Fisher Home—the same home from which I was adopted. I promised not to contact Diana until I heard back from him.

Even when I received Jerry's okay, I waited a month before calling. Rob, my husband, urged caution; this had the potential to be a tremendous joy or disappointment. "What if she's a beast? Or just doesn't want to see me? Or, what if Diana wants an ongoing active relationship—am I ready for that?" I asked.

I had spent a lot of time thinking about what to say. I didn't want to be confrontational, so I decided to introduce myself as the granddaughter of Gertrude Sparbeck. One morning, I pushed past my hesitation and called.

I couched the conversation tactfully. "I think I might be related to your family," I said to the woman on the other end of the line.

"How so?" asked the woman.

"I think I am related to Gertrude Sparbeck," I said.

"And I am your mother, and I've been searching for you for the past five years. You have three brothers, one sister, and eight nieces and nephews," she replied.

I was in shock! This was her! My heart was pounding, and a plethora of emotions filled my body. We spoke for over an hour. Diana had been nearby for all my life, even before it; Diana had attended the same high school as my father, she attended the same church that I did in Berkley, Michigan, and my mother, Agnes, had taught Diana's daughter in the fifth grade, the same school that I attended until sixth grade. Diana lived in Berkley as she raised her family, which was the next town over from where I grew up. She was a writer and wrote many poems as she travelled through her life.

The Casting Director

I was summoned with the message
There was a life He was casting me for.

I asked to see an outline of the script.
He showed me on a large overhead screen.
Seeing the demands of the part,
I wanted to back out.

Really, Sir, I don't believe I'm the type.
this life is really so challenging. I feel it
demands a more experienced soul to fulfill it.

I appreciate your concern,
I've already decided you're perfect for it.

But Sir, why all the abandonment, abuse, rejection?
I'm just starting out; a baby, a child.

I know—look how your spirit is surviving and loving.

Excuse me Sir,
You call this living?

Trust Me.

I want to, Sir, I admit I like the
(If you'll excuse the expression)
Hell-raising-rebel-activist-irreverent aspect.

I knew you would.

But God, why all the lessons?
Some repeated so often?

Trust Me.

May I see the next few pages, please?

Certainly.

Wow, that's great! I love this part.
Being pretty and smart, falling in love,
Being a wife and mom.
Look at all of those beautiful children!

Only some are yours to keep.

Why?

Trust Me.

How will I know what to do with them, and for them?

Trust Me. I'll be there—just love them.

Sir, all those extras playing different parts,
Why so many?

Lessons just for you—they all bring the gifts to learn
with.

Sir, would it be okay if I chose different parents?

Not really, they'll teach you the power of forgiveness.
Oh. I respect your decision, Sir—but do you think I
Can really handle the pain, the fear, the rage,
The guilt, the arrogance, all the ego stuff?

Trust Me—I'll help you grow through it.
I'll love you through it.

Sir, I know I'll be great with the fun stuff,
The magic stuff, the peace, the pleasure, the passion,
the Joy. I can really give that a lot of energy.

That's the easy part.

One more thing, Sir. Rumor has it there are
Superstar lives available, great leaders, spiritual
Leaders, that will touch the world and change it.
Would you consider me for a part like that?

I have. I've selected this life—it's yours.
If you choose, you can be part of changing the
World.
You have the only key—Love.
You just won't get top billing on that plane.

Diana Healy, June 14, 1995

Reading these words, I saw my mother's life through her own
eyes—full of struggle, resilience, and faith. It was a life that
had shaped me long before I even knew her.

First Miracle

My parents used to say they wanted me to be a nun.
I figured they meant it 'cause they were always
putting me in orphanages and boarding schools
run by nuns.

One Sunday, our parish priest came for dinner.
After grace, my mom said she "hoped and prayed I'd
become a nun."
Father Leahy said, "Save your prayers, they won't
have her."

That was the first miracle I ever saw, and
Father Leahy became my
patron saint.

Diana Healy, February 1974

When I reflect on this poem, I think about the parish priest
she talks about. I always remember my adoptive mother
Agnes talking about Father Leahy. Obviously, he was very wise.

CHAPTER 2
FIFTY-ONE YEARS PLUS BRUNCH

hesitated before telling my dad that I had found Diana. Would he be hurt? Would he understand? But I should have known better—just as he had my entire life, he supported me without hesitation. My sons, Kevin and Paul, reacted with caution. Still grieving their Mimi, they wondered—was Diana meant to replace her? And my brother John feared losing his only sister to this newly-discovered family. Despite their concerns, I felt ready to move forward.

Rob and I flew to Michigan from Boston to meet the woman who had given birth to me. During the plane ride, it all started to hit me. This was really happening!

We met at a beautiful upscale hotel in Rochester, Michigan, for brunch. I was very anxious about meeting Diana—my hands were shaking and my stomach was in knots. *Is this really going to happen*? I thought. I was fifty-one years old and never believed I would find her.

I saw a car pull up in front of the hotel, and a bellman helped her out. The bellman handed her a large canvas bag she brought along, and it appeared to be quite heavy. "I think that's her," I said of the flamboyant blonde woman in the full-length mink who entered the lobby.

She greeted me with a long hug, and I was stunned that this time had finally arrived. I introduced Rob to Diana. *Now, I wondered, how do we begin?* We were seated for brunch, exchanged some small talk, and then we began to dive in. I thanked her for giving me life. I was unsure of any resemblance, but Rob was thunderstruck by how much we looked alike, separated only by hair color and years. He even noted that we had the same mannerisms, like the way we folded our arms and the way we tipped our heads to listen. I was delighted to hear that I was 100 percent Irish; Irish, to me, signified joy and humor, and my parents celebrated Saint Patrick's Day every year with more than one hundred guests. We sang Irish songs around the piano for hours. My Uncle Charlie O'Connor, my godfather, whom I loved very much, was a proud Irishman.

Conversation began lightly, with photos of children and such, and then I and Diana traded our own histories.

As the day went on to what quickly became an eight-hour brunch, I realized that our years on this Earth may not have been as different as I originally thought. The differences and similarities became unveiled more with time. Time together with someone tells all as you relax and share your life stories. Time is what made me come to this realization and begin to appreciate our commonalities. Every moment of time is precious!

Discovery

Full speed ahead I thought
Get it all in an instant
I have to hurry and make up for all the time
I spent running away from me
Hurry! Hurry! Urgent . . .
There's not much time left
Then love came in and gave me just today
I slowed to the moment
And life and purpose
Began to unfold!

Diana Healy, August 1978

It's so interesting that when we are young, everything is always so urgent. I can imagine how Diana felt, finally finding her peace at twenty!

CHAPTER 3

OUR TWENTIES
THE DIFFERENCES LIFE
CAN BRING

By the time Diana turned twenty, she had already endured a lifetime's worth of hardship—emotional neglect, abandonment, and betrayal by those meant to protect her.

There were the little injuries: the eight-year-old Diana telling her mother, "I get to play the lead in the school play! I get to sing and dance! Will you please come and see me?"

Gertrude did not, neither did she go to see twelve-year-old Diana play Clair De Lune in a recital or see a fifteen-year-old Diana defend her school on the debate team.

"What's this about you getting the lead in the senior play?" Gertrude demanded of Diana at seventeen. "Why didn't you tell me?"

There were the deeper injuries: the backseat drives to the Sarah Fisher Home when she was simply inconvenient to them. Being touched by her paternal uncle, who swore her to secrecy. Even a vulnerable four-year-old Diana knew wrong when she saw it, and it must have been confusing and hurtful to be called a liar by her father.

There was the challenge and sadness of a sister with Down syndrome, who strained an already stressed family and was foisted upon Diana for care. Caring for her sister, navigating her family's expectations, and dealing with emotional neglect already made Diana's teenage years difficult. But nothing could have prepared her for the night that would change everything.

And then there had been the drive home from a party; an unexpected, unprovoked trauma that forever changed her life. Diana had gone to one of her friends' homes where they were having a party. They were only sixteen but considered to have a tendency toward the wilder side. They managed to find alcohol at the party and secretly enjoyed drinking and feeling the freeness of "just not caring!" As the evening went on, the parents realized that they were not acting normally, and after some investigation, it became evident they had been drinking. The parents were none too happy, and they asked an older cousin of her friend to drive Diana home. The ride home was not what she expected when he pulled over down a dark street and raped her. She never expected the trauma and everlasting consequences of that ride home. Diana was in shock but told no one. The violation was an awful, painful attack to experience. As the next few months passed, she realized that she might be pregnant. When it was confirmed and she told her mother, she endured not only the resultant disgust and embarrassment from her mother, but also the double-punch of both giving birth to me and letting me go.

After the rape and giving me up, Diana married Gerry Sarris in 1958 at age twenty. "Don't screw up a good thing by telling him about the child," urged her mother Gertrude, but Diana did.

Diana and Gerry struggled to have children; it would be four years before she gave birth to a daughter they named Laurie Ann, and she would have as many miscarriages over the years (five) as she did successful pregnancies. She wondered if this was some manner of Godly punishment for giving up her child. But still, she is forever thankful for her three sons: Chris, David, and Paul. The Sarris family enjoyed their lives together.

Diana was an exceptional cook. She loved making their house a home and spent much of her time focused on details that embraced love and nurturing. She loved their family's after-dinner bike rides. They would stop along the way and visit friends, or sometimes end the rides by swimming in their beautiful pool. She had such love for her children and joy for life. Our family now reflects often about her Irish humor, her love for music and dancing, and how special each holiday was, especially Christmas. She loved being their mother, but always felt an open wound for the child she gave away. As grandchildren arrived, her exuberance to share in their lives was so evident, and her presence was a wonderful memory for each of them. She would sprinkle fairy dust around so that they would know how much they were loved and that fairies were always watching over them.

As the children grew older, her professional life took off. She was working in a man's world of business, but Diana was an overachiever, and she excelled in her career in radio and later product sales. Maybe it was all that she had endured in her life that made her so focused and driven to be successful. She was an intelligent woman who was resourceful and resilient, and it was these two qualities that got her through the next trauma of her life.

Diana would divorce Gerry at about forty on the grounds of adultery, but she described him, long after the divorce, as a "bright spot in the storm." He was handsome, worked in advertising (an exciting field in the era of big-fin cars and newly miniaturized Zenith televisions that weighed under eighty pounds). He gave her solace at that time.

———— •• ————

Diana at twenty was no one's fool, and surely would not have been fooled by Ryan Knight. I met Ryan Knight in my junior year in high school, and we married in 1976. He was the handsome brother of my friend from Saint Mary's High School (now closed) in Royal Oak, Michigan, with its graduating class of fifty-two. I had struggled during those years a bit with weight, but otherwise enjoyed my high school years.

College would be the first of my shocks. Nazareth College may not sound intimidating; it had been an all-girls Catholic college. In the mid-1970s, marijuana was something hippies did and you saw on *Dragnet* reruns, but suddenly I was smelling it from under doorways. An all-girls Catholic college should be asexual, but it had just begun admitting men, and the women had already begun figuring out how to let the men in past security. I had been a happy, protected child and was left with no skills to deal with any of my new college experiences.

Besides which, I was in love with and distracted by Ryan. I wish I could say that the first choice in life, made entirely by me and of my own free will had been a better one.

Ryan was my best friend's brother, the older boy who had gone away to the military academy and turned up with great tales to tell around the holidays. He had been sent to the academy to calm his wild side, which did not work. As soon as he graduated, he began living with a woman ten years his senior.

He was not the sullen Brando-Esque bad-boy mystique. He had great tales to tell, tossed off one-liners with ease, and was one of those guys who could make a good party a great one. He also had piercing, handsome blue eyes.

Ryan returned home for a while, which was a joy; I had him nearby. I was taking the train back and forth from college, but found Ryan more interesting than nursing classes. Maybe Ryan knew he would marry me, but he began to think about his future and joined the Air Force. I should have been more aware of Ryan's betrayals when I received a phone call from a woman who was in basic training with him, claiming that she was pregnant with his child. It was a gut punch. I confronted him, and he said the woman was unbalanced and that there was no way that was possible. I was in love, and I trusted him.

The day I discovered that, despite all my parents' teachings, I was not special, was on a summer day in a little starter home outside of Oscoda Air Force Base in Michigan. Maybe I shouldn't have been so surprised about how Ryan treated me after his first betrayal. Even though I believed that the woman from basic training was not carrying Ryan's child, I suspected that he had been unfaithful. So nothing should have surprised me at that point.

Just three months married, Ryan and I lived in the small house on Loud Drive on a pretty man-made lake. We had been cleaning windows, me on the inside, he on the outside. I don't recall what I said to him—it likely was nothing much—rather, it was how I said it to him.

He put down his window cleaner and rag and walked calmly in the front door and closed it behind him. He slapped me, open-handed, across the face. I was still holding my cheek when he landed a punch to my midsection.

"Don't ever raise your voice so that our neighbors can hear you," he said.

Physical violence was not something I grew up with; I had been spanked once that I recall. By evening, Ryan offered the customary I-don't-know-what-got-into-me apology and promises not to do it again.

It is very easy to say now, "I would never stand for that," but a Catholic girl of twenty who believed marriage was for life, and who had truly loved her husband to that point, thought she could fix it somehow. It became my responsibility to keep the peace, and I kept the incident from my parents.

However, I managed to control my voice and my temper, but it meant nothing when Ryan drank alcohol. As time went on, he drank more deeply and more often; he did not require an excuse to drink. Most often, it would be slaps on the face, which would calm down before morning, or body blows with bruises to the ribs hidden by my clothing.

We lived in that house for a year, then rented another

house further out in the country. The calmer surroundings did nothing to calm Ryan, and one day, I had been hit one too many times and went back to my parents' house downstate.

My brother and father were furious, and my mother was terribly upset. Still, leaving Ryan was not on the table.

"You're Catholic," my mother reminded me very kindly. "You're married and you've made a commitment. Now, you need to get some counseling."

In hindsight, I don't know why I even tried counseling. Why would it be alright for someone, especially your husband, to hit you? The pain of the abuse weighed heavily on me emotionally.

Ryan and I first went to see our parish priest, who then sent us to a counselor.

Counseling went as counseling often does; it was fine, in theory. Ryan would be remorseful, would acknowledge that he overreacted to small irritations, acknowledged that drinking fueled his temper, and so on. The impetus to keep the peace was on Ryan, not me. This seemed to disturb him, but it did not stop his drinking. The abuse went on, but I put on a good front for my parents whenever we saw them.

We stayed at my parents' house one Thanksgiving, and we slept in my old bedroom. We had gone out that evening and got into some argument, which was loud in the car. We got into my parents' house and made our way up to the bedroom. Somehow, I got the better of him in that exchange of words, and he started punching me in the face. He was not in control of himself; every blow fueled him to throw another.

My mother burst into the room, took one look at Ryan with

his one fist raised to hit me, one bunching my dress below the neck where he grabbed me, and told him coolly, "Get out."

Ryan started to tell her what was and wasn't her goddamned business, but she stood firm. "Just stop, Ryan. Just get out. Now."

He paused a minute. Maybe he was trying to think of some way he wasn't a bastard and could not find it. He let go of my dress and bounded down the stairs and out of the house. My mother was in shock! I confessed to her that his abuse had been ongoing and that the counseling was not helping. He had broken my eye socket, something I did not know until I had an X-ray years later.

Thanksgiving came, with aunts and uncles and cousins as it always did, and I waited some time before I presented myself to everyone. Half of my face was swollen, and my right eye had a black ring. I don't know what my mother said to everyone, but no one said a word, and Uncle Chuck tried very hard to keep the mood merry; it was sort of his job, after years of doing it. I was embarrassed and ashamed that I was going through this abuse. The safety of my home and my family was a consolation to me. I stayed a few days longer, for whatever reason, just long enough to attend Ryan's father's fiftieth birthday party. Then I packed and went home to Oscoda.

Why was I doing this? Why did I even go to this party? I knew from my upbringing that this wasn't right. The abuse was frightening and unexpected. Ryan and I went to see the parish priest again, who put us in touch with another counselor, and I should have ignored them both and got out then. Ryan and I didn't have children yet, but I should have known better than to try to save the marriage. When I reflect now about the birth of my children, I should have considered what would happen to them in such a toxic marriage. I was too young and inexperienced and maybe even hopeful that we might be able to create a family. My sons, Kevin and Paul, were born two years apart and are a joy to me. We would be married for four and a half years before I filed for divorce. It was not about me anymore; it was about protecting the boys I loved and had brought into this world.

Some time, years later, I went to see Ryan's father at his tool and die shop. Ryan had stopped paying child support, and I wanted his father's help. There behind his desk was a family portrait from his fiftieth birthday party, which had a country western theme and had been the week after that fateful Thanksgiving. The makeup I wore did nothing to hide the swelling on my cheek or the redness in my bruised eye. All faces, even mine, smiled from under our cowboy hats. Of all the pictures Ryan's father had from the party, he had to display this one? I think Ryan's family was so impervious to the dysfunction of it all that nothing phased them. I didn't think that anything could get worse; I was so beaten down, but it did.

The final straw came on another holiday, a holy occasion.

Good Catholics that we were, we went to services on Holy Thursday, three days before Easter, which commemorates the Last Supper. We took part in communal penance, a form of confession. The idea is that unless you have a serious sin, you could be absolved in a group setting.

We drove away from the church afterwards, and Ryan was gripping the steering wheel and said in a strange voice, "I need to go back to confession. I have... a serious sin."

"Okay," I said.

I did not pry. Some moments passed.

"I planned to kill you," he said, and continued driving in silence. "My plan was that when you were in the bathtub, I'd drop a hair dryer in there to electrocute you. That way, we don't have to fight over the kids. I can have custody of them."

He pulled into a driveway to turn around, drove back to the church, and filled me in on the rest of his plan; the act itself, the finances, his explanations, his plans for the boys. I stayed silent, but I concluded then and there that I would get out and take the boys. His rage would not stop with me. They would be next.

I could have thrown some clothes in a bag and bundled the boys into a car and screeched off that very day, but I worried because we had bought the house from my father, who had bought it from my grandmother. I needed to get some help and advice, so I slept on the couch.

———— •• ————

If Ryan sounds like an animal, he was not. You could talk to him when he wasn't drinking. He usually wasn't drinking early in our marriage, and he usually was toward the end of it.

I began passing out. I would be in the kitchen cooking and crumple to the floor, or sitting in front of the television, and my eyes would glaze and I was out. My doctor speculated about neurological trauma, but believed it was plain old stress, and I agreed. I waited some days for one of those rare windows when I could talk to Ryan, and he asked me about the diagnosis.

"It's you!" I told him. "I can't pretend anymore!"

We had planned to separate while we tried to work things out, and Ryan promised to go to counseling again. I believe his confession of planning my death shocked him as much as it had me. But the years of tension and abuse and his confession at Easter were too much to bear. I asked him to leave, and he did.

———◆◆———

Go on and shake your head.

Ask me, "How in the hell could you have let it get so far? Didn't you see any signs that this was coming?"

Tell yourself, "I don't see myself standing for that," and "One slap is all it would take, I'd be gone, and that bastard would pay."

A good many of my friends have asked and said the same over the years, and I ceased to defend myself long ago. But I will do it, just this once more.

No, Ryan was not a problem drinker when I met him. He drank beer like any twenty-year-old does, sometimes less than others, sometimes more.

No, he did not expose himself as a batterer-in-waiting early in our relationship. He never struck me, and never even abused me emotionally, until we were three months married.

Yes, he had shown that he had a temper. He irritated easily; that same explosive energy he had in telling a joke would flip over into explosive cursing at someone on the highway, something he saw on television, or someone whose humor or politics he did not like.

Yes, he showed some signs of not being well-adjusted. He slept with a pillow held tightly between his thighs. I had to ask why. "My brothers and I slept in a bedroom in the basement," he revealed. "Two sets of bunk beds."

Boys with a bedtime of 8:00 p.m. just aren't done with the day, and they would play. Ryan's mother would slam open the basement door, pound down the stairs, and tell the boys that either they stay in bed or she would cut their penises off in the middle of the night. Ryan chuckled about her joke. "Surely, she had not meant it, would never have done it, and that hardly matters; she wanted us to believe it, and we were convinced."

Ryan's adult brothers slept with pillows between their legs as well. I was stunned that his family lived in a state of such chaos.

So, the alcoholism and the abuse did not announce themselves. They crept up on Ryan and on me. By then, we were married, which was something I took solemnly as a woman and a Catholic. No single incident seemed big enough to leave—not when the man was willing to seek help along with me. Time passes, the balloon goes higher, and it is more frightening to jump. Besides which, the abuse had become a kind of norm for me, as it had for Ryan's mother before me. His was a family in which a wife with a swollen cheek or a daughter-in-law with a horribly blackened eye were presumed to have spoken out of turn. In their eyes, it was nobody's business but the couple's.

I was pregnant with Kevin when Ryan's sister (and my high school friend) was getting married. I was supposed to be in the wedding, but I was seven months pregnant. It was late enough in the afternoon for his mother to be good and drunk and loose of the tongue, and she snorted. "You're so fat and ugly, if you weren't pregnant, Ryan would leave you."

Ryan defended me weakly, the way he always did against his mother. He had never had her love, and he was doomed to wait for it.

——— •• ———

I had been right that the boys would be next. They were next, both of them, once each, when they were older.

Ryan had taken a small apartment not far away in Birmingham, Michigan. He had not fought hard for the boys. Every other weekend, the boys and I would sit on the front steps among the backpacks and little suitcases, waiting for Ryan to come. Most of those weekends he did, but not always, and over time, eight or nine months would pass before he saw the boys. When he did, they would call me to check in, and I would ask them to put their father on the phone. "He's not here," Kevin told me, "He's gone to work."

I was in shock—they were only eight and six. I would drive to Birmingham to get them and leave their father an angry note, but he never argued or defended himself. How could I protect my boys? They were at such a vulnerable age and couldn't defend themselves. It was a worry, an ache I could not get over when they were with Ryan.

Kevin was nine years old and returned from a weekend

staying with Ryan and his girlfriend with bruises on his face and handprints from choking on his neck. This was why I always felt sick when they left me. He finally did what I had feared for so long. I was infuriated!

I tried to terminate his parental rights—Kevin had wanted me to—and was surprised by how strongly Ryan fought it. Ryan ended up with two or three hours every other week on a Sunday, which died out after a while because he simply didn't bother. He hadn't bothered either when they were toddlers. The fact that he fought me at all was surprising.

Paul was sixteen and living with Ryan in Michigan after I had moved to Massachusetts when he got his turn. After a few backhands and punches, Paul found a telephone and called me in a panic. I called my brother John and begged him to get over there and rescue Paul, which he did. Ryan lost his temper and beat up Paul, just swinging and punching him all over his body. It was unforgivable. I wish I could say that my boy came home to me, but he moved in with my brother John and his wife Jan. Still, he was safe. In four months, he went to live with his high school football coach and his family.

Call that unconventional, and it was. Paul found a father the way I had found a mother. He spent a year at his coach's house, with a man who gave a damn about him and a woman who influenced him very much. She was a nurse, a profession that Paul would ultimately choose. It was hell that my son didn't wish to be with me, but he chose a stable, solid place to be, and that was a relief.

That time was hell for me. I also lost my mother, and it took me four years to reach the point that I wasn't crying, that it did not dominate my every thought. My father remarried a year after my mother, Agnes, passed—my brother and I were not happy. These were very tough years. When would I find peace? When would there be a horizon of hope?

———•◆•———

Ryan found the right girl for himself; she watched both of these episodes with Kevin and Paul, but she still married him, and they had three children. Neither Kevin nor Paul went to their wedding. Kevin was fourteen when he found out his father would have another child. He was near tears, and said to me, "How can they have another baby? He's not even good to the children he has."

Eventually, Ryan was gone from my life, as well as the lives of his sons. "We'll make as much of an effort as he does," observed Kevin and Paul.

Labels Can Be Confusing

Years ago, I started out life as a soul
Then, as life passed through me and by me
I quickly began to gather labels

Irish, daughter, sister, Catholic, student, friend,
Girlfriend, fiancée, wife, mother, activist, alcoholic,
Hell raiser, free spirit, offbeat
And yes, career woman

That told the world who I was, and that's
How I played the life games—
Responding to those roles

My life became confusing and
The games became tiresome

All because I was distracted from my soul—
Which is my name, and the nature of my being

Diana Healy, June 1976

Diana was such a spiritual woman. As she grew older, it was apparent through her writing that she finally got to the essence of her being—her soul!

CHAPTER 4

A NEW YEAR'S CELEBRATION WITH MOM AND DAD

The soft glow of Christmas lights danced off a new ornament on my tree—a symbol of the year I found Diana. As I took in the familiar handmade decorations from my childhood, I thought of the love my mother Agnes poured into each one. And now, for the first time, a piece of my newly discovered family hung beside them.

This was our first Christmas since reuniting, and I wanted to give Diana something truly meaningful. I carefully put together a photo album—snapshots of my childhood, my high school years, and my own children. When she received it, she called me in tears. Every page was a chapter of my life she had missed, and now, at last, she could see the story unfold.

She was thrilled! She was thankful, and it truly was something she treasured. I knew how empty and sad she felt, that she missed all of those years. I couldn't think of anything more meaningful as a Christmas gift than this album for the woman who gave birth to me.

She always wanted us to get together whenever we were in town. She had such a sense of urgency about the importance of this for her. At times, it was too much for me. I wanted to take it slower so I wouldn't feel so overwhelmed. I called her when we arrived in Detroit for the holidays. As the holidays continued, Diana and I looked forward to the next milestone in our journey—our first New Year's celebration together. But this time, I had an idea that would make it even more special. I asked her if she would mind if I brought my dad with us to meet her. She was very excited about this, so I called my dad and asked him if he would like to join us. He was happy and honored to join, so the plan was set!

It was surreal for me to be with my birth mother and my dad. Thank goodness for Rob and all of his support. He was my rock, and his advice and strength helped me to embrace, enjoy, and explore all of these new experiences. As we sat together at brunch, I couldn't believe the moment unfolding before me—my birth mother and my dad, face to face, sharing the same table. Diana's voice trembled with emotion as she turned to my father. "Thank you," she said softly. "Thank you for raising her, for loving her, for giving her such a wonderful life."

My dad, always humble, smiled warmly. "Well, thank you," he replied. "She is a wonderful daughter."

My dad talked at great length about my mom, Agnes. He told Diana stories about growing up with a big extended family, my grandparents, aunts, uncles, and cousins. He recalled the memories of us all being together at the cottage on Lake Huron, the birthday parties, holiday celebrations, and overnights when we would swap kids between families. When all of the O'Connors, Binsfelds, and Crombes were together, we were twenty-five plus strong. Our childhood memories still are strong today and recalled by all of us on many an occasion.

Diana basked in hearing about the happy childhood I had. She felt comforted that she had made the best but hardest decision of her life. She shared memories of her children and their successes and the love she had for all of her grandchildren. She was finally at peace!

Later in the year, Diana wrote a letter to my dad. Here is what she said:

May 23, 2008

Dear Norbert,

I've written this letter many times in my head. The problem has been that I didn't know how to thank a hero and heroine. This is for Agnes, too. I don't believe I can express the love and appreciation I feel for the wonderful life you gave our daughter. From the moment she was born, she never left my heart and mind. The pain of not knowing how she was or where she was, was unbearable. The ever-asked question has now been answered. As her birth mother I could not have picked better parents. Julie grew up with love that was unconditional, warm, and inspiring. She is a brilliant example of all you two gave her. She loves you dearly. I am still basking in the miracle of having been reunited with her and meeting you, as well. Now I feel all the heartache was worth it. I know, thank God, that I made the right decision for her. And I am very grateful for that. So you see, it is hard to find the words to thank you both for all you did. You were in my daily prayers. Saying thank you seems little enough for everything. If you ever need a kidney you can have one of mine (a little Irish humor). Thank you, and May God Hold You In the Palm of His Hand.

> With Love and Gratitude,
> Diana

After meeting my dad, Diana felt a sense of peace, knowing she had made the right decision. But as much as our reunion brought healing, it also reminded her of the wounds of her own childhood. Years before, she put these emotions into words—words that now held even more meaning considering our reunion.

Showing Up

At eight years
Mommy, Mommy! I get to play the lead in the camp
play. I get to
Sing and dance. Will you please come to see me?
She didn't show up

At twelve years
Mom, Sister Zita told me I'd be featured in the
academy recital. I'm
Playing Claire De Lune. Will you and Dad come?
They didn't show up

At fifteen years
Mom, I was chosen to represent our school
on the debate team.
Can you please come?
She didn't show up

At sixteen years
Guess what Mom, I was chosen as a cheerleader.
Our first game
Is in three weeks. Can you make it?
She didn't show up

At seventeen years
"What's this about? You got the lead in the senior play?
Why didn't you tell me?"

Gee, Mom, I didn't want to give you the pleasure of
not showing up!

Diana Healy, 1974

I can only imagine this reflection from Diana regarding her childhood years—the pain and disappointment that she endured. Would she ever be able to forgive her mother?

CHAPTER 5
OUR THIRTIES
A HAPPY FAMILY AND
SAD ACCEPTANCE

In her twenties and early thirties, Diana fully embraced the spirit of the 1960s—a true bra-burning liberal. Despite her tumultuous upbringing, she was raised in a surprisingly tolerant household. Her parents had their preferences in music and literature, but they never spoke of differences or class distinctions.

Diana and Gerry were comfortable, he working in his ad agency she raising children and working in radio. She was a young mother and was always present at the children's sports, but she was different, the 'bohemian' and the 'free spirit.'

Diana was determined to be the kind of mother she didn't have. She wrote poems at the birth of each child. "I was confident knowing that someday I would receive the rarest of gifts," she wrote to her daughter Laurie.

"I am in wonder at your delightful soul, and I thrill to watch you live," she wrote to Christopher.

"Your wonder for life excites me, I love you, your possibilities are endless," she wrote to David.

To Peanut Paul, she said, "I'll tell the story about you showing up three months early, weighing in at less than two pounds, and how such a little guy fought such a big fight just to stay alive—the doctor called you 'Fighting Peanut Paul.'"

As her children grew, married, and gave her the joys of grandchildren, no birthday, school play, or holiday went by for Diana that she didn't share. She called herself the "Mother Bear," and earned it.

Diana struggled with alcohol and attended an Alcoholics Anonymous (AA) meeting, only to be turned away (she claimed). In time, she returned to AA and became a sponsor to a young man named Bill, who credited her with saving his life. This proved to be only one of the many people she touched in her life.

As Diana faced the collapse of her marriage and embraced a second bohemian phase, I was entering my own turbulent thirties, balancing single motherhood and a demanding career. I worked for my brother John's company, focusing on marketing and sales for statistical process control software, just like Diana, I was working in a man's industry, but like Diana, I was undaunted by the challenge.,

This work gave me an opportunity to learn networking skills, how to handle hard situations with customers, to travel for trade shows, and to build a business. I was a successful part of their team that opened doors for greater career growth later in my life.

At the age of thirty-four, I married Kyle Johnson; I had lost faith that I would meet anyone else, and again heard my mother speaking in my mind: *he's a good Catholic man*. This marriage was more of an intellectual than emotional decision. It was the kind of decision a survivor of abuse makes. The marriage lasted four years, but I describe it as a "blur in distant memory."

He was a staunch Catholic, active churchgoer, father of four, and, as I realized later, a sociopath. It took me a while to agree to marry Kyle. We met through my sister-in-law Jan; they worked together. He was a nice man who had been divorced and had custody of his children, who were all grown. At first, I thought that his intentions were good, but as time went by, I realized he was a controlling individual who lacked empathy and had no ethics. He thought nothing of stealing wood off the vacant lot across the street to use for refinishing our basement or benefiting financially from a salesperson's mistake. His moral character and judgment were a challenge for me, as I was brought up with parents of high integrity. I was less of a pushover for Kyle than I was for Ryan. When Kyle raised his hand against my son, something inside me snapped. I wouldn't be powerless again. Without thinking, I grabbed the nearest heavy object—a leaded frame—and hurled it at him. It was a moment of defiance, but it also made me realize how toxic our home had become. Still, the marriage trundled on—"Time goes on and you don't realize just how unhealthy the situation is," I said later.

During this time, I cared for my dying mother, Agnes. She had not been feeling well for a while, but didn't have a doctor anymore. She used to say that when her doctor retired, so did she from going to the doctor. I stopped by their condo every day on my way to work to check on her.

She was feeling worse and resentful of my dad. She was lying on the couch in the living room, and he was in the den watching TV, without providing her much help. It was evident she was getting weaker and weaker. I was finally able to get her an appointment with my dad's physician. Just helping her to dress and then walk to the car was an enormous effort. She was struggling so much, and my heart was breaking. My dad and I managed to get her to the office, but she was too weak to get out of the car. I went in to see what they wanted me to do. The nurse told me to take her to the emergency room at our local hospital. My mom had not stayed in a hospital since she gave birth to my brother John. She objected sternly, but we had no choice; she could not continue on in the condition she was in. We drove to our local emergency room, and they quickly moved her onto a gurney and into a room. I was so worried, knowing that all of this was so scary for her.

Things don't always move as quickly as we'd like, especially in a hospital. After an initial examination, the doctors called us into the room and told us that they thought her pain and discomfort was related to her gall bladder. Her eyes and skin had yellowed as well, and they admitted her for testing. When the initial test results came back, the doctor informed us that they needed to do a colonoscopy the following day. We were stunned to find out that she had been having bathroom issues with loose stools for about two years. This was a sad reminder for me of my grandmother, who had similar symptoms before she passed. I knew this was not good.

My dad and I arrived at the hospital early the next morning so we could be with my mom before the procedure. She was visibly shaken, and we tried to reassure her and calm her down. When the orderly came to get her, I leaned down, gave her a kiss, and told her how much I loved her. I could feel my eyes welling up with tears.

We headed to the waiting room, not expecting the colonoscopy to take too long. We were stunned when the doctor came out of surgery—it had been longer than we anticipated. He told us that my mom had a large mass in her rectum and they were not able to get the instruments past it. They took a biopsy of the mass and completed an emergency colostomy. We were shocked by all that had transpired over the previous few days. We stayed with my mom all day after she came out of recovery. We were uneasy about leaving her that evening, but they were giving her sedation medication to sleep. We would be back bright and early the next day. My dad left the hospital in the afternoon, and it wasn't until then that I spoke with the doctor. It was terrible news: she had rectal cancer that had metastasized to her liver. There was no opportunity for a liver transplant. The outlook was grim. There would be no chemotherapy, no surgery, no treatment whatsoever; the next step would be hospice. I met with my dad and John to inform them, as well. We didn't know how to tell her. My mother did not know the outcome of her tests.

Finally, after two days went by I spoke with her doctor and asked if he could convey the news, and I would be there with her for support. When the doctor came into her room, my father wasn't there yet, but we moved forward without him. My mom was in shock, tears flowing as she realized that her life on this Earth was limited. My dad arrived shortly after the doctor left. She told him what he already knew from earlier conversations with me, and he burst into tears as well. Forty-eight years of marriage. They had survived a lot over those forty-eight years, and their love was strong.

A few days later, we moved my mom home, and hospice came. They brought all of the equipment she would need: a hospital bed, care items for her colostomy, and medication to make her comfortable. At that time, I was still working for my brother John and his partner at their software company, so I was able to move my office to my parents' home and work there during the day. I would stay until early evening, get my mom settled, and head home to see Kevin, Paul, and Kyle.

My mom wanted to see her family and friends. John and I planned a beautiful party for her so she could see everyone and they could share their love for her with her. She lasted about six weeks—through the Christmas holidays—and passed in early January at 5:00 a.m. one morning with my dad, John, and me by her side. She was a young seventy-one-year-old, and I still miss her every day.

Kyle had resented my time away from home during my mom's illness. I phoned home and asked Kyle to get the kids (then in high school) off to school, and said I would tell them that their grandmother had passed later in the day. His lack of empathy was in full force that day, as he also stopped on the way to have breakfast with his friends before arriving to be with me at 10:00 a.m. That was my final straw with Kyle. I cancelled marriage counseling appointments, only to be told by the counselor that I should "run, not walk, from this marriage. The guy's a sociopath."

The diagnosis stunned me. That was a term reserved for people like Ted Bundy.

I was near forty and a single mother again, but I felt free.

Untitled

I'm in transition
It's exciting and painful
Laying aside familiar thoughts and feelings
And responses is scary
It makes me feel vulnerable
I was never comfortable with vulnerability

So, if at times I need you to reach out and touch me
Encourage me that I'll come through this whole
Please understand I'm not asking for a
Life-long commitment
I just need a few moments of your caring
Because sometimes
I doubt myself

Diana Healy, June 1977

Reading Diana's poem, I realized we were both standing at a crossroads in our forties. We had both fought for independence, battled through loss, and learned to survive. But now, we were searching for something more—for peace, for connection, for a soft place to land. And perhaps, in each other, we were beginning to find it.

CHAPTER 6

YOU'RE ONE OF US NOW

The conversations after the holidays with Diana were wonderful! Diana wanted us to meet her family, so Rob and I made plans to travel back to Detroit in March, which so happened to be the weekend our nephew had the lead in his high school play, *Oklahoma*. Great—we could accomplish two things! It was when we were on the plane heading back for this reunion that it started to sink in. Up to this point, I had been very grateful but guarded. I think Diana knew this. I just needed to take some time to adjust. For the first time, I was scared. I didn't know what to expect—I didn't know how her children really felt. Diana had told me that they were very happy for us. I just wasn't sure how I would feel about all of this if the shoe were on the other foot. The arrangements had been made—we were all meeting at Paul and Amy's house. Diana's heart sister and her daughter were there, as well.

Unfortunately, Dave and Karen couldn't be there, as they had a work commitment that weekend. We arrived at 6:00

p.m. with wine and flowers. Diana came out to the car to greet us. When we walked into the house, everyone was at the door waiting to meet me. She introduced me to them as their sister and Rob as their brother-in-law and the aunt and uncle to their children. Wow! They were all so welcoming! Chris handed me a beautiful bouquet of tulips (my favorite, he said they were Diana's favorite as well) and a crazy card signed by everyone. I'll never forget the inside of the card, which read "you're one of us now." They were shocked about the resemblance between us, and someone commented, "No DNA test needed here."

Here we all were—Diana was in heaven because she finally had us all together. She prepared a beautiful dinner of ham, pasta, salad, and the famous family cake. It was an intense night—they had lots of questions. Rob was fantastic and helped to set the pace so that I wasn't totally bombarded. We took lots of pictures and had our first opportunity to get to know each other. At the end of the night, it was just Paul, Amy, Rob, and me. Diana had left, as her back was really bothering her. So, Amy, in true Amy fashion as I've come to know, said, "So now what? Do we all spend the holidays together?"

She was right; all of this had happened, and we all wanted to know what all of this meant. They were worried about their mother being hurt. I was honest; I said I really didn't know what came next. I already had a wonderful family and family traditions in place. I was trying to figure it out, as well. Well, the four of us had a chance to talk, and I think by the time Rob and I left, we all were more comfortable. I didn't want Paul and Amy to think I was trying to take anything away from them or their brothers or sister or the rest of the family. This was a big change for me, as well. On the way home, there was a voicemail on my cell phone. Diana had left me a message about how much that night had meant to her; how she was finally complete—the missing person or piece of the puzzle was finally there. What we also learned that night was how warm and loving my new family was. I knew they had to feel somewhat cautious, but you would never have known it. We headed back to Boston on Sunday night—another memorable weekend!

Commitment

Really! Isn't marriage about mutual love, esteem, and affection
A choice to walk life's path with one's best friend
A mutual concern for each other's spirit and well-being
A bond of joy, loyalty, and strength that's nurturing and comforting
A space to grow; to feel free while looking on each other with confidence
A place where spirit grows and egos flee
And isn't it wonderful that each moment we are bound the choice is ours

Diana Healy, 1993

Recovery

It's over, I've survived, now I'm living, living free
I love it, I love me
My expectations quicken, I take delight in
all my senses
I know what it is to be turned on
All because I turned you off

Diana Healy, April 1977

As I reflect on how Diana must have felt being able to beat alcoholism, it must have been one of her proudest moments.

CHAPTER 7
LIFE-ALTERING

Our forties were life-altering for both Diana and me. With Diana's children growing, and her being a young-ish forty, she moved to Florida. She appeared to be recapturing her youth, which ended at seventeen, but may have been simply unraveling her failed marriage. Diana stayed in Florida with her daughter Laurie for two years. During this period, she traded her sedan for Laurie's red convertible and lived a free life, dating, painting, and trying to enjoy herself.

Diana took odd jobs in advertising and voiceover work and had a string of relationships. She wrote gloomy diary entries and poems about this time: "I think I miss not being able to share my joy with someone who deeply cares."

"You open the door for me and I'll let you know when your fly's unzipped."

She found herself open to men, but the relationships fizzled—one fellow was too Republican for her, another too stuck in his first marriage.

Diana moved back to Michigan and lived with her best friend, Val (whom Diana called a "heart sister") and Val's husband for two years. Feeling the emptiness of a failed marriage and the enjoyment of young children gone, she turned inward, and the weight of her young life crashed down on her. "Sometimes it feels like I'm running out of courage," she wrote.

But Diana's resilience carried her through as she began her recovery from alcoholism.

Years later, at about the same age, I married Rob Melanson and moved to Massachusetts to join him. Rob's childhood rivaled Diana's. He was born to a Japanese mother (Nana Yo) and an abusive alcoholic father. He beat Rob's mother frequently (and was jailed for it once), and it was completely characteristic of him to hurl the children's possessions onto the lawn and set them on fire. Still, all the hard punches he took as a boy didn't give him a hard outlook; they taught him to be protective.

Rob joined the Air Force and went to Vietnam. When he returned a year later on leave, he saw the bruises covering his mother. He told her that she must leave his father because he could not protect her while he was stationed so far away from home.

Rob and his family had little practice being close to one another. After being married to Ryan and Kyle, I was out of practice as well, but I recalled my mother Agnes's way of building a family. I encouraged Rob to invite his brother for dinner, and in time, Nana Yo spent weekends with the Melanson family. Meanwhile, I again drew closer to my sons,

Kevin and Paul, now in their twenties. Their relationship with me had been strained during their teenage years, but with the pain of relative abandonment by Ryan long past, Kevin and Paul came to appreciate my support during those years. In time, the Melanson family grew more tightly knit, much like my childhood family.

Diana would observe Rob when she met him: "Finally! A son-in-law I can love."

She stated that if I had met Rob when I was younger, it never would have worked. I was too Republican for him, he too Democratic for me; his family life was small, mine was giant and Catholic and Irish. It was not the first marriage for either of us, but it endured.

My forties were a time for major career growth. I started working at a small venture capital-backed company named Sensitech as an inside salesperson. At that time, we sold temperature monitors that the food and pharmaceutical companies would use to monitor the temperature of perishable or temperature-sensitive products while in transit. As guidelines and requirements for both industries evolved, so did the need and desire to ensure that products were being maintained at proper temperatures. The company was focused on growth, and for years, we successfully doubled our annual sales. During the early years, I moved quickly into new positions; from inside sales to specific product sales, which required a lot of travel, to territory sales for the food division, to regional, and eventually, director of food sales. At that point, our focus had shifted to not only providing temperature data for our customers but also aggregating that data, analyzing it, and providing recommendations for improvement in temperature performance of their supply chain. A new department was created called "Professional Services," and I worked hand-in-hand with the gentleman who started it, which was exciting. We were both successful; I was focusing on the sales part of the solution, and he, with his expertise in food safety and cold chain, worked on the information and recommendations. Professional Services was a critical decision for the company and it set us apart from any of our competition. When I started working at Sensitech, I was employee number thirty-seven, and by 2016 we had over 1,000 employees and were well over $250 million in sales. Our growth was organic and through acquisition. It was not only a great company to work for, but the people and my team made almost every day a joy! In 2013, I took over the Professional Services team of forty personnel as vice president. As our customer base and sales grew, so did the team that supported those sales. When I retired in 2022, my department was worldwide and with over 150 people comprised of data analysts, data management, program and project managers, client and technical services, and training.

Throughout these professional growth years, our children also grew into educated, hardworking members of society. All are now married, and four have children of their own. We are very proud of our five children and their life partners; we always look forward to enjoying our family, and especially our eight grandchildren, during retirement!

Take It Back

I want to love you, Mother, but first I want you
to take it back
All the "if onlys," the limitations only you designed
for me
The name calling—emotionally unstable, possessed
by the devil, clumsy,
Un-lady-like, juvenile delinquent
Take back wishing you never had me, the hopelessness,
the jealousy, the fear
Of your stuff, and knowing one day I'd discover how
frightened, lonely, and
Stuck you were
I want you to take back all of the things you said and did
that planted fear and rage
In an uncluttered spirit
You can't now and probably never would have, it's
okay though, you know,
Because I followed a different voice than the one
I heard
Somehow I knew to do that
The funny thing is
I love you anyway

Diana Healy, 1974

How awful to hear such horrible things when you are a child
and hoping to thrive and grow into a well-adjusted contrib-
utor to society. They say it's easier to raise a child than heal
an adult. So true!

CHAPTER 8

OUR FIRST AND LAST MOTHER'S DAY

Diana had yet to visit me in Massachusetts until she decided to do so over Mother's Day Weekend in 2008. It was a coincidence that it was Mother's Day. I was hesitant, but Diana was not. "Don't leave me alone with her!" I begged Rob, since our talks were intense, and pushed my comfort level.

I had come to recognize that Diana was obscuring her financial situation; she was working part-time selling advertisements. Rob and I considered sending Diana the plane ticket for her trip to Boston, but Rob recognized that this would hurt Diana.

Meanwhile, my bonus daughter Renee was enduring a difficult pregnancy; she was confined to bed rest in the hospital, and Rob and I had to take our granddaughter Mia home for the weekend. The situation, I concluded, was our family's life, and Diana should see it as it was for all of us. I was happy to note that Diana was immediately comfortable.

Rob picked Diana up from the airport and brought her to our home. We loved our beautiful house that sat on the Merrimac River in Amesbury, Massachusetts. We were fortunate to live in a beautiful area where there was a state park across the river. It was not uncommon to see eagles flying down the river. We loved the nature, the kayaking, and the walks.

We introduced Mia to Diana. Diana was excited about spending time with Mia and our family. Diana insisted that we stop for a moment to pray for Renee and the well-being of our new grandchild-to-be. We were very proud of our home, and we were so happy that Diana felt comfortable visiting. At one point, Diana saw a photo of my dad with his second wife Sarah, whom Diana had known as a young woman. She said, "I can't stay in this room with that picture; she is evil in that picture."

Diana's ability to assess people was very keen and I was surprised that she could grasp the sense of who Sarah was from just a photo.

The weekend was a combined celebration of Mother's Day and Mia's third birthday. Diana and Nana Yo, Rob's mom, took to one another. It was so amazing for me to see my mother-in-law, whom I loved dearly, with my birth mother. I now had an abundance of mothers. The family gathering was memorable; everyone except Renee and her husband was there, and we had a wonderful celebration of Mia's birthday and Diana's visit.

I grew more comfortable as the Mother's Day weekend passed, and I took Diana to the beach in Massachusetts while Rob took Mia home to Renee. Diana was unafraid to delve into the details of her life, but I had been more guarded. I let down my guard and revealed to Diana that I, too, had been raped at thirty. I said it in one sentence.

I reflected that once I had heard my father was Diana's rapist, my childhood ideal of the star-crossed professor and student romance was more than gone. My own experience was with a man I had dated, 'The nicest guy!' by everyone's estimation. He had grown impatient, as the relationship had not reached the sexual stage, and liquored me up one night at a party and raped me. I became pregnant and had an abortion, in contrast to Diana, but the two women, years apart, made their own decisions. The abortion haunts me more than the rape.

Diana's reaction was quiet. "I just can't believe it," she said, "I'm so sorry."

The entire conversation with Diana was all of three sentences. We shared this experience, and we both survived.

I had told my mom a few months after it had happened— the guilt of the abortion that followed was unbearable. I was afraid to tell her, expecting some brand of Catholic rectitude. I underestimated my mother, who held me tightly. If she held any judgment, she felt my suffering and knew I had paid already. I was not a schoolgirl like Diana when it happened. I was thirty, divorced from Ryan, and my boys were six and eight.

At age thirty, I was perhaps better equipped to cope with my rape experience than Diana had been at seventeen. Maybe not emotionally better equipped, but I was in control of whatever that decision was going to be and wasn't going to be influenced by anyone who tried to force that decision upon me. I had done what Diana refused to do, but what we had in common was that we made our own choices.

——————•·——————

I reflect upon the nature of motherhood, comparing my own experience with my mother Agnes to that of Diana's mother Gertrude Sparbeck, as well as my own experience with my father's second wife, Sarah.

"How come you say to me 'I love you,' then you go and leave me any time, any place you feel like it?" Diana had written to her own mother when she was nine years old. "Don't you ever, ever, ever tell me you love me again . . . I'm going to spit in your face and kick you real hard."

My experience with my adoptive mother, Agnes, was the diametric opposite of Diana's. A teacher by trade, my mother, Agnes, was the kind of woman who made people feel heard and cared for. She was very much the heart of the family and left a gulf when she passed. My mom always made you feel that you were the most important person in the room when she was talking to you. She always remembered what you were talking about, and if you were troubled, she would check in later to see how things were going.

Within five months of my mom's passing, my dad began dating Sarah and would marry her less than a year later. Sarah and her deceased husband were acquaintances of my parents; she was one of the very few people my mom disliked. I graduated high school with Sarah's oldest son. Sarah considered herself a good Christian, the type to volunteer at hospitals.

However, she was also the type to blurt out something unkind, like, "Your father never really loved your mother."

Sarah was unexceptional, unlike Diana. They were the same age, but she had none of Diana's spirit and love.

She observed coolly that Diana was 'bohemian' as a young woman. Living in the same community, they met and socialized when their children played in Little League.

—————•◦•—————

Maybe I expected my personal story about my rape to somehow comfort her. We shared this experience, and we had both survived.

Diana and I had about three hours alone together at the beach, and then headed back to our home. Rob had already returned. When we entered the house, he had a strange look on his face and said, "A curious thing happened when I got home."

He said that he took our golden retriever Molly into the backyard to play, and oddly, he kept seeing smoke at the end of our long driveway. He decided to see where the smoke was coming from, so he took the long walk to the end of the driveway. Looking up and down the road, he couldn't see where the smoke was originating. Turning back toward our house, Rob saw flames coming from under our porch. He ran to connect a hose and was able to put the flames out. It was quite a scare—if he hadn't arrived home when he did, the scene could have been quite different. Diana and I were in shock! Rob said it appeared that the mulch was set on fire, and then the porch lattice started to burn. We realized that when Diana was smoking out on the porch, she was flicking her ashes onto the new mulch, which then caught on fire. The damage was small, but she was tremendously embarrassed and apologetic for what we felt would be a forever funny family Diana story. She begged me not to mention it to my half-siblings. The story was so good that I had to call Renee and Kevin to share it. The rest of our day was quiet, and Diana left the following morning. Her first visit to our home was filled with wonderful talks and shared times that gave us such fond memories.

———————————

Diana would telephone persistently, and the calls were long, which was difficult for me, a professional woman having to manage my time.

I at last wrote Diana a letter, observing that we had years to get to know one another, and asked if we could take things a little slower.

Friday afternoon
June 20, 2008

Dear Diana,
What a wonder it is that I was able to locate you last year. It truly is an amazing story. It has been a pleasure over the past several months to get to know you and your family, learn about family history, and see so many similarities between us.

It was great to have you out here with us for the weekend. I'm enclosing some pictures I thought you might enjoy. That Mia is really something else! Thanks for being so patient and understanding—I was glad to hear that you thought she added to the weekend! Life does not always work out as planned. Thanks also for all the gifts! The angel holding the child, the books (I've started The Princes of Ireland), the drinks (Rob enjoyed every sip, me too), and just the sharing of your heart. It was all wonderful.

You know, after we talked yesterday, I was thinking. I want you to know that I do appreciate that this experience is very different for each of us. I know that giving me up was a very painful time for you and the subsequent years carried a continuation of that ache. I know that I've told you this before, and I hope you are happy to hear this: I never felt abandoned. I only felt love from my parents and brother; I never 'felt' adopted. My mother was wonderful in how she explained how much you loved me and how it must have been so hard for you to give me up. When I think about that and the fact that it was the 1950s and '60s, she was really pretty progressive. Anyway, she was right—I did have a birth mother who loved me very much, and the act of giving me up truly was a selfless act. I can only imagine how hard that was for you, but I am very grateful that you made the decision you did. I have wonderful parents, brother, children, and family.

I do want to tell you, though, that I feel that I disappoint you sometimes—I'm sorry for that. My life is so busy with work, children, and grandchildren that I don't always have the time I'd like to spend with family and friends. This is an ongoing challenge for me, but one that I've just had to accept.

I also realize that you look at things from the perspective

of my mother—you have lived with this for fifty-plus years. For me it is a little different. I love you for giving me life, and I am very happy that we have reconnected. I think about the years ahead of us and the times we will hopefully share and look forward to those.

Unfortunately, the reality is that I live in Massachusetts and you in Michigan, and we both have busy, active lives. I feel pressure if I am not always able to respond as quickly or have as much time as you would like. I know that you would never want me to feel badly—but I also know that I am very conscious of how you feel. I just needed you to know how I have been feeling. Time will provide us with opportunities to get to know each other better and share more of life's experiences.

I also want you to know that I have talked to my brother John. He is fine. We've had a chance to talk often lately and he understands why finding you was important to me. He is very supportive. Hopefully, this summer you will have an opportunity to meet John, Jan, Katie, and Jon. They are just all so special to me—I've only had one brother to share my life with and he knows me very well. I'm sure, just like the bond between Laurie, Chris, David, and Paul—I think it's a sibling thing—you share so much.

I'll talk with you soon. Thanks for listening.

Love,
Julie

I hoped that Diana was not disappointed. Diana phoned immediately, saying that I could not possibly disappoint her. She reflected upon the "miracle of having been reunited with me and meeting my dad, as well."

Diana sent me a poem she had written years before. Giving me up had haunted Diana for decades; it was "the most absolutely horrible thing she ever experienced."

DEAR KIMBERLY MARIE, MY POEM FOR YOU WITH SOUL-FILLED LOVE

Always the questions, my soul haunts me with every moment, always there, no matter what else I am doing.

Where are you? Are you happy? Have the Angels somehow let you know how much I love you? Are you tucked in bed with a hundred fairy kisses and beautiful stories? Do you feel happy? What is your favorite food? Do you like to run very fast? I did, it brought me joy. Do you love to laugh and giggle? Do you do that often?

What is your favorite color? Do you love to dance? I do, every day. What color is your hair? What color are your eyes? Mine are blue, and my hair is dark auburn. It saddens me to think you will never know this. You will never know how I search every little girl's face that I think looks like me and wonder, *Is she my daughter?*

I pray every day you live in a wonderful home with fantastic parents who show you how special and wonderful you are.

I can only have faith that God watches you tenderly. Today I was taking the sheets off the clothesline and the kids and I were smelling them (we love to do that), and I wondered if your mom hung your sheets outside so you could smell the sunshine, the breeze, and the clouds in them as you lay your sweet head on your pillow.

I miss reading to you, hearing you laugh, fixing your favorite food, and kissing you goodnight and good morning. I miss taking you shopping and special just you and me lunches. I miss hearing you say, "I love you, Mommy." I miss planning your birthday parties.

Darling daughter, my precious child. I will miss you all the days of my life, and I will always feel that you are missing. I trust you will grow up to be a loving, empowered young woman; I count on that, and somehow it brings me comfort. Giving you up for adoption was the most absolutely horrible thing I ever experienced. It will always haunt me. It is my faith in God's Grace and Love that you are loved and well.

I love you bigger than the Earth and heaven,

Mommy XOXOXOXOXOXOXOXOXOXOXOXOXO

Diana Healy, 1960s

Wait a Moment

> **Excuse me life, would it pose a problem**
> **If I asked you to slow the pace for a moment?**
> **I'm learning that all I need and want is found in the moment,**
> **And I just discovered that a lifetime is in the moment.**
> **So could you ease up just a little?**
> **I need to savor my discovery.**
>
> **Diana Healy, April 1970**

I can only think that Diana appreciated every moment, every memory she had . . . that's what seems to happen as we grow older.

CHAPTER 9

AS WE MOVE FORWARD

Over the next few weeks, Diana and I spoke and planned a time for us and our families to get together at our cottage on Lake Huron. Rob and I were taking our usual two-week vacation back to Michigan. As always, there was a lot of preparation and anticipation of being able to spend time with my family at my favorite spot in the world. The weekend before, we usually started the process of pulling everything together: golf clubs, clothes, Molly's food and toys; it was a busy time. Interestingly, I tried to call Diana the Thursday before, but she didn't answer her phone. I left a message, but did not hear back. I commented to Rob, "It's so strange that I haven't heard from Diana, she usually calls me right back."

Sunday afternoon, I went upstairs to my home office and noticed that I had three missed calls. When I checked the voicemail, they were all from Chris asking me to give him a call and that it was important. I immediately called him back.

He told me that Val had been trying to reach Diana as well, but couldn't, so she decided to take a ride out to her apartment in Rochester. When she arrived, she could see Diana's car, and through her window, noticed that Diana's purse was still on the counter. Val immediately called Chris, who, in turn, headed to Diana's house and called the rest of the family. When Chris arrived, he and Val called the police so they could do a wellness check. The police came and went into the apartment. They found Diana in her bedroom, lying in bed—she looked peaceful. They believe she had passed sometime on Thursday based on her condition.

I was in shock! Chris told me that they would like for me to come to the funeral, "Of course," I said. "Let me talk to Rob, and I'll call you right back."

Rob was stunned as well. We decided to pack up the car and start heading to Michigan right away. I called Chris and told him our plan. He said, "The funeral home is going to let the family see her before she is cremated, and if you can make it by Monday night, you will be able to see her as well."

I told him Rob and I would be there.

I called Kevin, Paul, Renee, Evan, and Sam, and they couldn't believe what I was telling them about Diana. My next call was to my sister-in-law, Jan, to share the sad news and see if they would mind us staying with them. As usual, Jan said, "Of course not!"

John and Jan were surprised as well and realized this would be a very hard time for me. Both of them were nothing less than totally supportive during the emotional days that followed.

———•——

I reflected that I was suspicious about Diana's health.

Diana had strode into that first meeting at the hotel, all signs of vigor, but over time, her frailty revealed itself. She left the first meeting of her own children and me because of back pain. She passed out at a part-time job she was working about a month before she died, and was taken to the hospital in an ambulance. Her doctors advised that she stay the night for testing, but Diana defied them (and her sons) and went home in a cab.

I believe that Diana knew she was dying. She had told Chris that she dreamed she had met her mother, Gertrude Sparbeck, in heaven. "I'm not done healing," Diana protested, but Gertrude (speaking more kindly than she ever did in life) told her, "You can do your healing here."

Diana reflected that a seventy-year-old woman should have felt more at peace, but her life had always been a path toward peace, rather than peace itself. Diana was found lying in a kind of repose, wearing a gown, her limbs at rest, and a drop of blood in the corner of her mouth. Likely, she knew her time had come.

———•——

Rob and I returned to Michigan for the funeral. For the entire two-day drive, I wept constantly, to the point that it frightened our golden retriever, Molly. "I'm not a crier," I declared, but I was crying for fifty-one years of loss.

We arrived at the funeral home, and thank goodness, our son Paul came with us; Kevin was out of town. It was my first time meeting my half-brother Dave and his family. Also, it was the first time that our son Paul would meet any of our new family members. It had to be one of the hardest times I've ever gone through.

Diana, my mother, the woman who gave birth to me, was lying in peace. The moment filled me with emotion. Diana was so strong that she endured the hardest thing she could and gave me up. We all spent about ninety minutes at the funeral home. We prayed as a family for Diana and ourselves as we headed into that heart-wrenching time. Afterward, we all went to my brother Paul's house for food and bonding time, as we needed to console each other for our loss. The funeral home gathering was the next day.

Memo To: Me
From: Me

Be loving and enthusiastic about yourself
and life around you.
Only then can you take from life what life
is waiting to give you

Diana Healy, 1977

This is such a simple reflection, one that Diana must have realized that some of us never do.

CHAPTER 10

SAYING GOODBYE

G rief is hard enough without feeling like an exhibit. Several hundred people attended Diana's wake, but I was the one they whispered about—the lost daughter with Diana's face. I wanted to mourn, but I was also a stranger in that room; someone to be examined, pointed at, and compared to.

I met so many people at the wake who loved Diana and her family. So many people would just walk by and point at me, obviously seeing the strong face resemblance to Diana. I loved that I looked like her. Rob often commented about how Diana and I had mannerisms so similar to each other. In the short time that we had together, I recognized that I was blessed with her resilience, expressiveness, drive, and love of family. I met a man at the funeral home. I can't remember his name, but he was also adopted and found his birth mother. I asked him how his adopted mother felt. He said, "She was very happy and supportive," and that she told him, "You can never have too many people who love you."

As overwhelming as it was, her wake was a reflection of all the people who loved her and who she had touched somehow in their lives. Diana's children introduced me as one of their siblings, and Chris touched me by asking me to join them to meet with a priest and arrange the mass. During the funeral preparation time, Chris asked me if I would like to see Diana's apartment, since he was heading there to gather some of her things. "Of course," I said.

I wanted to see, hear, touch, and feel as much of Diana as possible.

Diana lived far more modestly than she had let on. Diana wanted to project success, wearing a mink to that first meeting at the hotel and treating everyone to brunch, declaring herself a "millionaire in the making;" but in fact Diana had lived very modestly. This may have been the only time in her life that Diana had hidden the facts; she appeared to have feared disappointing me. Diana presented her book of poems with great pride. There was a small life insurance policy (I was not a beneficiary, to my relief), and a second policy which was ultimately denied because Diana had not been open about her medical history.

Diana was more spiritual than religious, but her funeral was a beautiful mass at Dave and Karen's Catholic church. After the mass, while gathering outside, Rob and I saw Bill, the young man whom Diana had sponsored in Alcoholics Anonymous. He was married, owned a successful landscaping business, and told us that Diana saved his life. It was a time for reflecting about my birth mother and remembering how beautiful her soul was. The three of us were talking, along with my dad and his wife, Sarah. Sarah just spat out, "You knew the good Diana. I knew the bad Diana," a comment that puzzled me and infuriated Rob.

Well, that stopped that conversation, and we all headed to Diana's celebration of life. In the car, Rob was so angry and he could not believe what Sarah had said because it was so inappropriate and served no purpose but to disparage someone who was loved by many. That was just the beginning of a dreadful, nasty week at Lake Huron with my dad and Sarah.

Diana's celebration of life was a large, warm, wonderful gathering at the country club where Dave had a membership. While Rob and I were driving to Michigan, I had an opportunity to write something that I wanted to say to everyone who had gathered:

July 2008
"And I am your mother…" Those are the words I heard when I first spoke with Diana last October. And so it began; my relationship with the woman who gave birth to me on May 15, 1956. "Miracle" is the word that she and I used to describe our reunion.

Diana withstood unbearable pressure during a time in society when unwed mothers were ostracized—when giving birth outside of marriage was less forgiving. She told me over the past several months how she knew one thing at that time—that she was going to have this baby—me. I knew then and learned more over the next several months that this is how Diana lived life: with conviction and passion!

I was her first of five children, the one she only met for moments in the hospital, the one she would not know until over fifty-one years later. She called herself the "Mother Bear," and that she was. Her love for her children and grandchildren was unparalleled! When we reconnected, my husband Rob, my sons Kevin and Paul, and I were automatically part of her family love den. This brought many benefits: her devout prayer life, her special connection to God, her protective nurturing nature, the simple pleasure she received from the joys in our lives, and her ability to share a piece of that Irish mind of hers . . . how I'll miss all of this.

Diana and I spent our first Mother's Day together this year at our home in Boston. It was a relaxing time for us to get to know each other even better. We shared memories, good and bad, over the past years. Diana was always so grateful to my parents for the life I had, and we prayed together when she was there to my mother, Agnes, who passed almost twelve years ago. Agnes had always told me when I was growing up, "Your mother must have loved you so much to give you up."

She was right—my mother did love me; she loved me and missed me for fifty-one years. Diana and I didn't have as much time as we would have liked together, but the time we did have was remarkably memorable.

Diana has left me with another gift. Laurie, Chris, David, and Paul—you are a beautiful reflection of our mom. In you, I have found her warm-hearted, welcoming nature and love of family and friends. I learned so much about you, your spouses, and your children even before we met from the many talks that Diana and I shared. She loved each of you uniquely—each of you brought such joy to her life!

Mom, I need to tell you again: thank you for giving me life! I will miss you—miss getting to know you better—being able to share those mom/daughter talks. I'm so grateful that God brought us together! I know you are still with me and I will carry you in my heart always.

From one Irish lassie to another: May the road rise with you and the wind be always at your back and may the Lord hold you in the hollow of His hand. As Mom would say: what happens now, it remains to be seen.

Ego

Since the time I can remember, I've heard about how
we are all born with Original Sin
I heard how the soul is pure when it awakens in Earth
school
I've read a little about it, it was certainly drummed
into my head, about MY Original Sin
Hearing about it sometimes made me feel unworthy
of God's love
Theologians have spent countless hours studying it
Religion uses it to frighten and demean people
When I grew up I dismissed most of what I heard from
my religious educators
One morning when I awakened, my soul spoke to me
Original Sin is EGO
It's a tool we use to connect with our soul
It's not a stain, it's a gift
I believe God loves us past the pain of the Ego, our
Original Sin
God is good and wise

Diana Healy, 2008

Diana spent her life searching—for love, for meaning, for connection. She wrestled with faith and doubt, with ego and surrender.

After we found each other, she wrote this poem about ego, saying it stood for "Easing God Out."

She was right. And yet, I think she finally let God in.

CHAPTER 11

INTRODUCTION
TO MY ANGST

S arah and Diana's lives had briefly intersected many years ago when they were two young mothers in Berkley, Michigan. But as I would later learn, knowing someone and truly understanding them were two very different things. They belonged to a group of parents, mostly women, who were acquainted through Little League.

The first time Diana and I talked, I told her my mother, Agnes, had passed, and that my father had remarried someone from Berkley named Sarah Gatlin. Diana said, vaguely, "I knew Sarah and Pat Gatlin."

Sarah was equally vague about Diana. "She was kind of a Bohemian," said Sarah. "She had that free spirit."

Sarah described the Sarris kids as nice kids, the family a nice family, and that Gerry Sarris was perhaps the more serious of the two.

I knew Sarah because her son and I went to high school

together. She and her husband were acquaintances of my mom and dad, whom I'd see once a year at the annual Saint Patrick's Day party.

Once I graduated from high school, that would be the only time I saw them; then not again until I was thirty-nine and my mother was dying at home. It was two days before she passed, but my mother could go at any time when Sarah arrived and announced that she wanted to talk to my mother. She and my mother had been casual acquaintances at best. My mother lay in her sickbed, not very alert, and in her nightgown.

"Now's not a good time," was the best way I could put it. Sarah insisted, arguing with me that she and my mother had known each other for years, pushing back on all my reasoning. I stopped reasoning with her, and stood in the doorway with one foot touching either door jam, and said, "No. You can't come in."

It had not occurred to Sarah that my mother may not have wished to see her, and it hardly mattered.

Truth be told, my mother had liked Sarah's now deceased husband just fine, but had never cared for her. It was very rare for my mother to speak ill of anyone, and it was memorable when she did. My mother approached people with kindness; Sarah approached like a barge, demanding to hear their stories and inserting her opinions at will. "No filter," Rob would later declare.

Guarantees

I don't recall how I missed the guarantee stamp
No ninety days or one year tagged on my life
I kept looking for them on everything
I saw and felt that it was good
But I wanted more than ninety days or one year
I wanted a lifetime guarantee
And the pain
Of not having it hurt a lot
One day after I'd been here awhile
I figured out that when you're under construction
There are no guarantees

Diana Healy, June 1977

Diana was always a learner until the day she passed on. She loved new things and new experiences. It's so evident in this poem she wrote. We are always under construction until the day God calls us home.

CHAPTER 12

A WATERSHED MOMENT

The five months after my mother passed, my dad kept himself busy sorting through her possessions and learning whatever tasks she had always done, and so on, but one day it got to the point that he knew he had to go on with life. His first step forward was to phone Sarah. It was a watershed moment.

The first summer that Dad was dating Sarah, I thought, *Please don't have her up to the cottage on the weekends.* It was the first summer after Mom had passed, so it would be strange enough without her there and twice as strange for someone else to be there in her place. Still, Sarah was up every weekend, and my brother and I were horrified.

"Dad," I told him finally, "you can have her up any time during the week. Please don't have her up over the weekend," which was when John and I would be there.

That was a hard talk to have, and we had it twice more, but in time, Dad finally heard us. Then he married Sarah, and of course, she was there as often as she wished, usually cleaning out whatever she thought was worthless.

Sarah is the kind to bite off half a chip with one dip and use the other half to try another.

"Please don't double dip!" I begged her, only to be informed with a wave of her hand that I was being ridiculous. I stopped serving dip.

Call me petty, but there was this little fork; my grandmother's "picky fork," I called it as a girl, the kind you use to eat shrimp, that I loved. Whatever hors d'oeuvres I was serving one weekend at the cottage, this ancient (probably valuable) silver "picky fork" would be the perfect addition.

"Where's the picky fork?" I asked her.

"Oh, I threw that out," Sarah informed me.

"Sarah," I said, with as much control as I could, "You do whatever you want to do in my dad's condo, but you don't touch anything in this cottage."

"But . . ."

"Don't touch anything up here. Nothing."

———— •• ————

John and I were in our forties, and Sarah was hardly a 'New Mommy.' Still, you expect some sense of reverence.

"You know," she confided in my brother John one weekend at the cottage, "I don't think your father's very smart. I think he talks numbers because that's what he's comfortable with, but I don't think he's very intelligent."

"He was smart enough to invest well and improve her life dramatically," I told John later.

As horrifying as Sarah's comment was, it was not the most horrifying one that she made. However, our father seemed happy, and we resigned ourselves to tolerate and anticipate Sarah's rudeness.

I tolerated it, but I was not at peace with it.

My sons were careful when they dated a girl to keep details from Sarah. They were wise to do so; they knew that Sarah had no qualms about digging her heels in until she unraveled the mystery of someone's family business. At my own wedding, she grilled Rob's mother, Nana Yo, about her divorce: "Why did you do that? Come on—details!"

Nana Yo politely demurred and kept demurring the harder Sarah pushed her. "I just don't think there's anything wrong with that," Sarah sniffed when we challenged her behavior.

Knowing my mother, Sarah's continual prying into the lives of others was what annoyed her the most. In a Catholic family, family business stays within the walls, and you reveal whatever you wished about yourself, but not about anyone else. Knowing Diana, that was what annoyed her about Sarah, as well. As she put it often about gossip, "It's not your tale to tell."

Two years after Rob and I married, we were living in an antique home that had been built in 1728, and my dad and Sarah travelled from Michigan to visit. It was a comfortable old place, with a central chimney that heated the whole house. We ate dinner in front of that fireplace, and Sarah was surprisingly pleasant, talking about Dad and something he'd done that was thoughtful. Whatever it was, it was fairly trivial, but it was kind.

"Yeah," I said. "I'm sure he did that because he realized after my mother passed that there were a lot of things he maybe should have done or wanted to do and never did, and decided he wouldn't make that mistake again."

"Well, your father never really loved your mother," Sarah declared.

She must have recognized the look on my face because she repeated what she'd said and went on with her examples. I stared at her mouth moving for a few moments before I got up from my chair and went into another room to sit down with my head in my hands.

Sarah came and found me and got down on her hands and knees in front of me, so I could see her. She was pleading with me to understand that "He loved her, but he was not in love with her."

"Get out of here!" I barked at her.

———••———

I found my dad the next morning, while Sarah was in the shower.

"Dad," I asked him outright, "I need to ask you this question: did you love Mom? Were you in love with Mom?"

"Absolutely," he said.

Not a moment's thought about it. Still.

To My Children with Honor

Mother's Day is nearing,
Tradition encourages us to honor mothers
I'm taking license with this day, I
Want to honor you

For all the laughter and joy—
Running footage in my heart
For the lessons you taught me—
Our growing pains
For the wisdom you helped to me to reach for

For moments of firsts
First steps, first words, first haircuts
Cuddles and the smell of baby powder
Rocking you to sleep
Tucking you in for the night
Lullabies and popsicles and high fevers

For watching you explore, laugh, discover, learn,
wonder, and share

For campfires at the beach
For the runny-nosed kisses and little hugs
For all the "Love ya, Moms"

For all the crayon pictures and pasted cards
Stored in my own Louvre
For the times my heart got caught in my throat—
Just looking at you

For all the faithful moments
Trusting me
Having patience
Tolerance
Understanding
Acceptance
Forgiveness
For mistakes I made

For coming through problems, divorce, life, solutions,
death, joy
For staying bound together
As a family with love

For humor, wit and practical jokes
For having generous hearts and noble spirits

For loving me, accepting, and supporting me
For celebrating me with your love
For making my life more beautiful
Than I ever expected

I honor you with LOVE

Diana Healy, 1994
For Laurie, Christopher, David, and Paul

Diana had written this poem for her children, but as I read it
again, I realized how universal its message is. She understood
the power of love, of family, and of the small moments that
make a life.

And so, today, I take the liberty of devoting it to my own five children—Renee, Kevin, Paul, Evan, and Sam. Thank you for your love, your laughter, and your acceptance. You are my greatest gift. Family is love.

Passports

> When I ponder the gifts I want to bestow on my children
> One of the most important is a passport
> A passport to their feelings
>
> I want them to seek passage
> To explore every emotion
> To observe, learn, partake in the journey
>
> Particularly the feeling that appears dangerous
> Anger, abandonment, loneliness, guilt, shame, sensitivity, and yes, vulnerability
>
> I want them to know if they think
> "Warning, danger zone"
> They can enter and safely travel through it
> Because they have the courage of great spirit
>
> I want them to understand, the journey is required
> To reach their homeland and freedom
>
> Diana Healy, 1995

Isn't this what every parent wants for their children? Diana was superb at understanding and expressing what the journey will entail.

CHAPTER 13

AND LIFE GOES ON

G rief doesn't end at the funeral. It lingers in the quiet moments, in the unexpected gifts, in the realization that someone you loved is now just a memory you carry.

Chris arrived at the cottage holding a small, beautiful box. Inside were some of Diana's ashes, along with a few of her belongings. The box was adorned with a carving of a child kneeling in her mother's lap—a symbol of what we shared, and of what we had lost.

My emotions were raw, but I held the box tightly, grateful that a piece of Diana would remain with me. It was something I would always treasure.

As a new family, we continued to stay in touch over the next year, and Chris reached out to tell me that Mom had wanted her ashes spread over Houghton Lake, but they thought it would be more meaningful to spread them over Lake Huron at our cottage. He asked, "Would that be okay with you?"

I was so touched and thrilled to tell him, "Yes, it would mean the world to me."

We planned a day when everyone in the family could be there, and we all sat in a circle of love on the beach, each expressing our love and thoughts about our mother. We gathered to collect part of her and walk into the waters. With such respect, devotion, and love, we all gently laid her in the beautiful, calm waters of Lake Huron that God had created. She is at last in her final resting place, right where she wanted to be!

We spent the rest of the day celebrating her; her love of life, her family, her Irish heritage, her passion, her Catholicism, her humor, her womanhood, her determination, her resilience . . . just HER.

WITH THANKS

So, my conception and birth were not tales of star-crossed love. My birth mother had been restless and a bit of a wanderer who had struggled with alcohol. She was a remarkable woman, but a challenged one as well.

I am grateful to Diana for having given me up; it would not have been an easy life for me if she had raised me. I never felt like I missed out on something; my adoptive family was loving, and they were mine.

Diana was remarkable, but my adoptive mother, Agnes, was remarkable as well; her funeral was as large as Diana's. A memorable moment for me was a fifty-year-old woman and former student giving me a yellow rose to place in the coffin for all the students Agnes had touched.

I often reflect on how much I was influenced by both mothers: Agnes through her nurturing, and Diana by nature. I inherited Agnes's sense of family, but Agnes was not a survivor in the way that Diana had been—she did not need to be. I believe that my strength in surviving two abusive marriages and a rape (among other challenges) was somehow derived from Diana. I wonder if somehow Diana's words to me as a newborn were advice and warnings and lessons which somehow took. I have felt a guiding hand through the years; one which helped me to endure the battery in my first marriage, defend myself mightily in my second, and find peace in my third.

I am grateful to both of my mothers, the one who raised me and loved me, and the one who, fifty-one years later, had a chance to show me her love again.

Karmic Debt

I accept the spiritual fact that this life is about
Payment of karmic debt without question,
Save one

Couldn't I have been given naturally curly hair
While making the payments?

Diana Healy, 1995

Diana's humor was unmatched! She always had a funny way of looking at life. I'm sure it was one of the things that helped her survive.

To Our Casting Director

Our lives took solo paths
From the moment of my birth
Two souls separated by age and whereabouts
Two souls who trusted You.
Sir, you guided us through pain, heartache,
abandonment,
Abuse and rejection over the years
We trusted You to help us, and You did.
We lived every moment of the time You gave us
Even when we wanted to give up
We trusted You and we survived
We laughed, loved, succeeded, and enjoyed our happy
days,
That was the easy part
We created our families, our children, and tried our
best to
Give them love, stability, and the tools to live the
lives You gave them.

Sir, next, you gave us the rarest of gifts, each other,
again.
We trusted You to guide us with Your grace and
Lead us to a place of love and understanding.
You, Sir, took our hearts and opened them so we
Could take in the lessons we learned along the way
And share these wonders of life with each other.
We prayed that You would walk with us
along this time, and You did.
You gave us eight months to share
Our children and families, Diana and me.
You kept me safe even in times of apprehension

You gave Diana the tenderness to let me experience her.

Sir, you asked us to trust You
The trauma of losing Diana once again
Was almost too much to bear
I knew You were guiding me through this time
Thank You for the peace I finally achieved
Thank You for the time we had together
Thank you for my family and the new family I have.
Thank You for the mothers who loved me so much
You have led me through life with Your most
Important gift—Love.

Julie Melanson, 2025

Our Meeting Day
November 11, 2007

Brunch with Diana, my dad, Rob, and me
January 1, 2008

My mother Agnes

Nana Yo and Rob

My new brothers and sister
Paul, Chris, Laurie and Dave

My brother John and my "sister" in law Jan

Diana and her sister Debby

Debby, Diana, and Laurie

At our Lakehouse in Michigan with
My new niece Baillee, my new sister-in-law Amy, Me,
and the rainbow of Diana is visiting in the background

Ome and Healy —
my writing support group

Childhood photo of my family

Rob and my children
Evan, Sam, Renee, Paul, and Kevin

Melanson wedding family photo

The Perfect Ending Healy Pass, Ireland

ACKNOWLEDGEMENTS

As a new author, there are many people who have been instrumental in assisting me in writing this book. First, I would like to thank my author coach Shannon Hazel; my editor, Valerie Costa; my first readers (you know who you all are) for all of your constructive feedback—you helped me to see my story through your eyes. Thank you to all of you who endorsed me and recognized the heart and soul I put into this writing. To MFL, the attorney, who reviewed my content. To my daughter-in-law, Maureen, for always helping me to find the right person for the legal support I needed. To my niece Katie for your technical support and knowledge in helping me to "pull it all together" and expertise in marketing. To my cousin Moe, who travelled with me to Ireland so that I could experience the beauty and essence of my family history at Healy Pass. Simply—thank you!

ABOUT THE AUTHOR

Not all adopted children get the chance to discover where they come from, but Julie Melanson did! Her journey to reconnect with her birth mother, Diana, revealed unexpected parallels, heartbreaks, and triumphs. With raw honesty, love, and compassion, she tells a story of resilience, identity, and the enduring power of family. Julie Melanson emerges as a promising author driven by a compelling personal narrative.

Julie is an up-and-coming author who has lived a tale that most adoptees would never have expected. She has sadly experienced the love and loss of two mothers, after which she was compelled to tell the story of both of these wonderful women who shaped her life in different ways.

Beyond her budding career in memoir writing, Julie brings a wealth of experience as a retired vice president of a cold chain/supply chain visibility company, where she dedicated twenty-five years of her professional life.

Residing in Michigan, Julie cherishes her proximity to water, a lifelong source of inspiration, alongside her husband Rob. She and Rob live close to her family, which includes two grown sons, Kevin and Paul, and three bonus children—Renée, Evan, and Sam—whom she loves as her own, along with eight cherished grandchildren.

In her leisure time, Julie finds solace in reading, golfing, and treasured moments with her family. She shares these moments with Ome and Healy, their beloved Portuguese water dogs, who are loyal companions in her daily life.